WHO
Shall Roll
Away the Stone?

Alan Jenkins

**Grosvenor House
Publishing Limited**

This book is published by
Grosvenor House Publishing Ltd
Link House
140 The Broadway, Tolworth, Surrey, KT6 7HT.
www.grosvenorhousepublishing.co.uk

A CIP record for this book
is available from the British Library

ISBN 978-1-83975-903-1

DEDICATION

This volume is dedicated to the many who have helped me along the Christian pathway in so many ways and in so many different circumstances. May the blessing of God be their reward for such gracious support.

Many thanks,
Alan Jenkins

PREFACE

In every generation in human history there have been crises, which have challenged individuals, groups, communities and nations. In these situations, those involved have had to resort to measures, either of their own resolve and implementation, or to a higher source or authority, with power to execute the necessary action to resolve the situation.

When such human endeavour fails there is the conscious realisation of dependence on a power, outside of themselves, a supernatural power, on which they instinctively call for deliverance or resolution. Such power belonged to the "gods" who exercised that power, as considered appropriate.

Such was ancient belief and it is still with us in this present century. The contents of this book are intended to show that those listed, were women and men who faced immense challenges, in crisis situations, with impossible odds, but achieved success through dependence on "the true and living God", who by His infinite power removed the "stone" which barred the way, and effected deliverance and provision to enable the individual to achieve the aim set down.

These examples are but a chosen few among the many faithful servants of God, who through generations have proved by experience that the God they served is both powerful, present and faithful in keeping His promises.

INTRODUCTION

It is Mark who records in his gospel the question, among the women, as they made their way to the tomb to anoint the body of Jesus, who shall roll away the stone? This was something that apparently came into their thoughts as they made their way to the tomb, since the main focus of their endeavours was that of the traditional ritual of anointing the dead body, albeit in this case a special body, that of the Lord they had come to know and love, who had left so many memories of healing, comfort, relief, restoration, help, guidance, instruction etc. and had so cruelly met an end so degrading, so distressing, so ignominious and humiliating.

This was a ministry that uniquely belonged to the women who had followed him and now sought to show their devotion in the only way available to them, that of anointing the body, which had been withheld from them, because of the sabbath. (Mark 16:1). Talmudic tradition indicated that the burial of the dead ultimately rests with the whole community. These women took responsibility for executing the duty, relating to burial, as laid down in the scriptures.

Although much care was undertaken in the preparation for the anointing, one factor remained unaccounted for, THE STONE, a barrier which they, as individuals, could not overcome, but they were to see something beyond their expectation when they arrived at the tomb, for behold, "they saw that THE STONE was rolled away, for it was VERY GREAT" (Mark 16:4).

LIST OF CONTENTS

Rahab and the spies.
(Source: public domain)

CHAPTER 1

RAHAB THE HARLOT

Whilst people, in general, look upon the outward appearance of individuals they associate with, the scriptures tell us that, "God looks upon the heart", the inner being, the person, stating categorically that, "the Lord sees not as man sees" (1 Samuel 16:7).

When we consider the life of Rahab there in Jericho, we tend to look at her through eyes that see a harlot as the scripture declares and conclude that she was an "immoral woman". Whatever the case is, and it has caused much debate, and whatever the opinions formed, and they differ in many aspects, one thing is sure GOD SAW what people could not see, and therefore for Rahab the question was thus answered, "who shall roll away the stone?" And what a stone it was, if we may borrow the words of Mark, the gospel writer, and say, "for it was very great" (Mark 16:4).

The fact that Rahab was well known in the city and its surrounds is confirmed by the scripture record, "the king of Jericho sent unto Rahab" (Joshua 2:3). Word of her actions and dealings reached the ears of the king, who was duly concerned about the consequences of her actions.

Urgent, even immediate, plans had to be formed to alleviate the wrath of the king and the threat to the lives of Rahab and those of her family, for she had mother, father, brothers, and sisters, who were open to the wrath of the king.

Such a crisis required a resort to everyday practice, common to the culture of the day, that of lying to the messengers of the king so that her actions could not be discovered and her family made safe. (G. Morrish, in his dictionary says, "her falsehood is not commended but her faith is" (see Hebrews 11:31).

Here another stone was to be removed and hence a later prayer (request) (see Joshua 2:12) for a token (pledge) of truth (Bullinger, *Companion Bible*, indicates, "the earnestness of the appeal") that her family would be "preserved" when it was all over.

Here we see in action the faith that God alone could see in the heart of this immoral woman (so called) that would ultimately, not only deliver her and her family from death, but elevate her to heights, the like of which she would never have dreamed of. Rahab was witness to, and recipient of God's goodness and grace. Such is the testimony of scripture which declares that Joshua SAVED Rahab the harlot alive and her father's household (see Joshua 6:25).

But better was to come. The Divine record shows that Rahab was not only saved from destruction but entered a new life among a people, chosen by God for blessing, and in which she would be part of a new family, which would lead to the birth of a greater SAVIOUR than Joshua, even the SAVIOUR of the world (Matthew 1:15), great David's greater son.

Hannah in the temple with Samuel.
(Source: public domain)

CHAPTER 2

HANNAH, MOTHER
OF SAMUEL

Hannah was a pious and God-fearing woman, married to Elkanah, who had a second wife, named Penninah. Hannah was childless whilst Penninah had children, and exploited the situation and provoked Hannah, making her life a burden and unfulfilled, to the extent of weeping and sadness from which she could not be comforted.

Her only resort was to seek the Lord that He might resolve the situation and remove what seemed an insurmountable barrier. Who could roll away this "stone" but God alone? Though Elkanah was sympathetic and sought to relieve the situation it was not sufficient, and with the provocation of Penninah and the inept judgement of Eli, to say nothing of the wickedness of Eli's sons in their dealings in the temple, Hannah was completely cast upon God to resolve her desperate plight.

Once again, we see that man's extremity is God's opportunity, and through prayer Hannah prevailed, because God heard her prayer, "and remembered her" (1 Samuel 1:19). Hannah's next visit to the temple was after Samuel had been weaned, this time to declare to Eli, not only the answer to her prayer, but the fulfilment of the vow made in her prayer, to "lend" the child to the Lord "as long as he lives".

Not only had the "stone" been rolled away but a new vision embraced, which would lead to a life of service to the Lord and his people, but also blessing for the nation in the anointing of a shepherd boy who was to become their greatest king and the forerunner of the "King of Kings, even the Messiah of Israel. How true is the scripture "the earnest prayer of the righteous avails much" (James 5:16)?

Many a voice has been heard to declare that Hannah was lacking in compassion and was unwise to do what she did in leaving Samuel with Eli in the temple. Her yielding of her firstborn to the Lord was no mean act of duty, nor just the keeping of a vow, but one of complete and utter trust in the God, who had made possible the one thing she desired, above all earthly treasures, that of bearing a son.

In her song of thanksgiving she declares, "there is none so holy as the Lord... none beside thee... neither is there any ROCK like OUR GOD" (1 Samuel 2:2). "The pillars of the earth are the Lord's, and He hath set the worlds upon them. He will keep the feet of His Saints" (1 Samuel 2:8 & 9).

Hannah's trust is implicit, her confidence is unassailable, and her hope impeccable, her ROCK is immovable even the GOD of ISRAEL. The God and father of our Lord Jesus Christ.

Ruth meets Boaz.
(Source: public domain)

CHAPTER 3

RUTH THE MOABITESS

Ruth was brought up in a pagan society where the most feared god was that of Chemosh or Molech and was constructed to enable child sacrifices to be executed by a consuming fire. Such was the background against which Ruth was raised before she came to know the God of Israel. The story is related in the book of Ruth, when Elimelech and Naomi emigrated to the land of Moab, with their two sons, Mahlon and Chilion. The move proved to be disastrous as, within a short time, all three men, Elimelech, Mahlon and Chilion, died leaving Naomi and her two daughters-in-law to fend for themselves. The time came when Naomi decided to return to the land of Israel, telling her daughters-in-law of her intention and her inability to secure a future for them, and exhorting them to return to the land of Moab and seek husbands that they may find rest and security. At this critical point, decisions were made by Orpah and Ruth, Orpah deciding to return to Moab and Ruth deciding to cleave to Naomi and go with her to the land of Israel. The pledge of Ruth, as recorded in the book of Ruth, is very moving and is indicative of Ruth's commitment to Naomi and more importantly to the God of Israel.

The law of Moses, as recorded in the book of Deuteronomy chapter 23 verse 3, that no Moabite was to enter the congregation of Israel, "for ever". Here was the stone that appeared insurmountable for Ruth, and could only be removed by the grace of God.

So it was that Ruth went with her mother-in-law, Naomi, to the land of Israel and they came to Bethlehem in the beginning of barley harvest. What was to follow was quite incredible as God worked in his own way, to fulfil his purposes, even with this Moabite woman, to bring her into such a privileged position, as the grandmother of the great King David and the lineage of the future Messiah.

Many bridges were to be crossed before Ruth could find herself in such a position of true blessedness, but God's will was to be worked out in her life, and Naomi was to witness the goodness of God as a "restorer of life" (Ruth 4:15) so that out of death there in Moab came life in Israel and future posterity.

Esther before the King.
(Source: public domain)

CHAPTER 4

ESTHER THE SAVIOUR

Esther's early life is blighted by the loss of her mother and father, thus being an orphan, and having to be brought up by her cousin, Mordecai. Due to circumstances beyond his control, but divinely ordered, Mordecai, in obedience to the king's commandment, allowed Esther to be taken to the king's house, and put under the supervision (in the custody) of Hegai, the keeper of the women. Thus, the preparation for the "rolling away of the stone" was begun.

The beauty of Esther was to enthral the king, and eventually she was brought in before him. He fell in love with her and she obtained grace and favour, so much so, that she was made queen instead of Vashti.

In the course of time, as Mordecai kept vigil of the palace activities, and in particular of Esther, he heard of a plot to assassinate the king, told Esther of the plot, who then informed the king and the king's life was preserved. The details of the event were recorded in the annals of the kingdom. Now the king's chief advisor was a man named Haman, an Agagite, who exercised great influence in the court of the king and beyond, even amongst the people, so that all bowed down to him. But Mordecai would not do so, causing Haman great distress. Upon discovering Mordecai's identity with his people, the Jews, Haman set about the destruction, not only of Mordecai but all the Jews in the kingdom.

Haman connived the permission of the king to issue a writ to undertake the killing of all Jews in the kingdom. When Mordecai heard this, he rent his clothes, went in sackcloth and ashes, and cried in the city, making known the decree regarding his people in the kingdom. When Esther heard this, and received instruction from Mordecai, she was faced with a momentous decision as to what to do.

Not even Esther, privileged as she was, could appear before the king with a request, without the king's permission, and to do so would put her life in peril. Esther, because of the magnitude of the crisis, decided to appear before the king, on pain of death, if she did not obtain the king's favour, in order to put her request. Who could roll away this stone, but God himself?

Thus, she went, obtained favour in the sight of the king, and the rest is history. Haman and his plot were exposed, and he was hanged on the gallows he had prepared for Mordecai; Mordecai was promoted and became great in the king's house, the Jews were delivered by order of the king, throughout the kingdom, and an annual feast was inaugurated to celebrate the deliverance, which is kept to this day, and called Purim.

Mary Magdalene.
(Source: public domain)

CHAPTER 5

MARY OF MAGDALA

Mary Magdalene was foremost of the women which followed Jesus and is mentioned in the four canonical gospels more than any other of the group of women who ministered to him. Much has been debated about her character and manner of life, but details in the gospel records relate only to the fact that it was her demon possession that brought about her notoriety and the record shows categorically that it was, "out of whom the LORD cast SEVEN DEMONS" (Mark 16:9; Luke 8:2).

This deliverance executed by the Lord was, in effect, the removal of the stone which had proven to be so great a barrier in the life of Mary and enabled her to launch out in a ministry, as a devoted follower of Jesus, that continued through to the resurrection of Christ and beyond. Secular history seems to indicate that she was a woman of means, but her physical condition i.e., demon possession restricted her activities until her deliverance, hence her great devotion to her Lord. Thus says the scripture, "unto whom much is forgiven the same loves much" (Luke 7:47). Mauria Casey, author of *Jesus of Nazareth*, surmises that Mary must have suffered severe emotional or psychological trauma, being battered and bruised, injured and in agony from the suffering demon possession entailed.

The gospel accounts mention the presence of Mary Magdalene (Matthew 27:55 & 56; Mark 15:40; John 19:25) at the crucifixion, whilst Luke mentions the women that followed him from Galilee.

Such was her devotion that she remained at the cross to the end and then followed those, who took down the body, to the tomb of Joseph and saw how his body was laid in it (Luke 23:55). How fitting, then, that Mary was to be among those to, "view the empty tomb", the stone having been rolled away. Yet again the challenge that faced her as she made her way to the tomb, had been removed, though she did not fully understand the implication of such a revelation.

Still reasoning in her mind, on a natural plane, she thought that the body had been stolen, "they have taken away my Lord and I know not where they have laid him" (John 20:13). Thus, she spoke to the angels, having declared to the disciples the very same thing. (John 20:2).

Here we have one of the many "twofold" statements that occur in the gospel of John (an interesting study starting with John 1:14 & 17 – e.g., GRACE AND TRUTH – two being the number of WITNESS).

Such was her devotion that Mary returned to the sepulchre, when the disciples had returned to their homes, and stood weeping and, as she wept, she looked into the sepulchre (John 20:11). Two further revelations were to be her experience on that eventful day. Firstly, to see two angels in white, one sitting at the head and the other sitting at the feet where the "BODY OF JESUS HAD LAIN". Mary was again to reiterate the statement, "I know not where they have laid him" (John 20:2 (we) and 20:13).

Human reasoning always reaches a limit, where divine revelation gives the answer. John tells us that when she had thus spoken, "she turned herself back" and "saw Jesus standing". Yet another revelation was needed, this time when she turned, she heard and knew his voice and responded with the word "RABBONI" (Master). What an indescribable blessing to hear and know HIS voice. (John 10:3 & 27).

Thus, was fulfilled her deepest joy, to see and to hear her master in "resurrection power". Obedient to his command, "go to my brethren" she came and told the disciples she had seen the LORD and he had spoken to her (John 20:18).

This woman who had known possession by demons now experiences, not only conversation with angels but dialogue with the risen LORD in resurrection glory. What a transformation, what a unique experience, what a wonderful privilege. Thus, she passes from the scene, content in the knowledge of resurrection power and glory, with a confident faith and anticipation of faithful promises yet to be realised. Thus, the stone had truly been removed.

Ann Judson of Burma.
(Source: used by kind permission of Wholesome Words –
www.wholesomewords.org)

CHAPTER 6

ANN JUDSON, BURMA

Ann Judson was born into a religious family, her father being a deacon at the church in Bradford, Massachusetts. She was a popular and attractive young girl, with a zest for life and social activities and a regular attender at the local Congregational church.

It was at this time that Ann began to consider seriously what was the basis of her life, and the revival taking place at this time set the stage for Ann's conversion. Earthly vanities and indulgences were becoming less consuming and spiritual realities more convincing, as the Spirit of God brought to bear the folly of trifling, passing earthly joys.

In the year 1806, on a visit to an aunt, she discussed her feelings, burst into tears, and was tenderly told of the gospel of Christ and duly gave her life to Christ, publicly confessing him as her Saviour, subsequently both her parents, brother and sisters were all converted. Thus, the first stone was rolled away to open up a vista of exercise regarding service for her newfound Saviour.

She writes at this time of her desire to live to the glory of God and sets her mind to improve herself for his glory. (*The life and Significance of Ann Hasseltine Judson (1789–1826)*,

Sharon James, *Journal of Missions,* Southern Baptist Theological Seminary, SBJME 1/2, 2012).

On 5 February 1812 Ann married Adoniram Judson and on the nineteenth of February, some two weeks later, they set sail for India. After a short while they were ordered out of India by the British East India Company and in July of 1813 they moved to Burma, Ann having a miscarriage aboard ship. Yet another challenge was to be met, as they had been told that Burma was "impermeable" to Christian evangelism.

Ann, with her husband, devoted much of their time to studying the language, taking some three years or more to speak it reasonably fluently. Contact with the homeland was non-existent during this period, but undeterred, they persevered and accommodated Burmese customs and sought to open their home to the people. It was from these early beginnings that a church was formed and converts gathered as the work grew.

In 1922, due to ill health, Ann had to return to America where she used the time of furlough to write about the missionary life, which writings became widely read in America, and brought about a great interest in mission work for many years. On her return war broke out between Britain and Burma and the Burmese put all English-speaking foreign men in prison, and so Adoniram was imprisoned as a spy. Such were the conditions that he barely survived in what became known as "the death prison".

Ann faithfully visited him at the prison on a daily basis, praying for his release, and pleading his case before Burmese officials. Who could remove the stone but God alone and orders for Adoniram's release came because the Burmese government needed an interpreter in their negotiations with the British and Adoniram was ideally suited for the position. Upon his release Ann's health grew stronger and yet again the stone had been removed.

It was while serving as an interpreter that Ann's fever returned and, in her weakness, passed away on 24 October 1826, leaving Adoniram broken hearted. A few months later, baby Maria also passed away, adding to the despair of Adoniram.

Adoniram continued in the work of the Burmese mission, planting many churches, and completing the translation of the Bible into Burmese. Ann's contribution, in translation work as well as ministry amongst other secular commitments, left a legacy that continues to this present day, proof of the power of God to roll away the stones of resistance, opposition, difficulties and challenges to leave open opportunities for the advancement of His Kingdom.

Fanny Crosby, poet and hymnwriter.
(Source: public domain)

CHAPTER 7

FANNY CROSBY,
THE BLIND POET

Fanny Crosby was born on 24 March 1820 about fifty miles from New York city, the only child of John and Mary Crosby. She was, by religious conviction, a Puritan, and a member of the exclusive "Daughters of the Mayflower".

At less than ten weeks old she was diagnosed with eyesight damage, which it seemed was congenital, and became blind, and when she was six months old her father died, so she was raised by her mother and maternal grandmother, both of whom were dedicated Christians. Thus, she was instructed from an early age in the stories and principles of the Bible.

Very early in life she began writing poems, her first being at the age of eight. Thus began the removal of the stone, which for some would have been an insurmountable barrier, but for Fanny was a means to greater achievements which, for one so young, was a dream that was to be realised in so many ways.

She set her mind not only to reading, but memorising the scriptures, so that from her mid-teens she had memorised the four gospels, the Pentateuch, the book of Proverbs, the Song of Solomon and a number of the psalms.

In 1834 she enrolled in the New York Institute for the Blind and was there for eight years, as a student, and two further years as a graduate pupil. During that time, she learned to play the piano, organ, harp and guitar, as well as becoming an acceptable soprano. Thus, were laid the foundations of a life of service for her Lord and Saviour.

Her first resolve was to repay the Institute for their care and education and she undertook to travel and teach grammar, music and poem instruction on their behalf, which she found rewarding, and successful, though demanding, and eventually caused health problems requiring a time of rest. She returned to the school and engaged in teaching and occasional poetry writing.

In 1858 she married Alexander, a teacher at the school and together they pursued their individual careers until Alexander's death in 1902. Fanny had a special place in her heart for the poor, and in order to minister to such she went to live in the run-down, crowded apartments, of the city. Her writing of poems and hymns was becoming more widely known and a number of different publishers were keen to take up her talent and publish on a regular basis. One such publisher was Sylvester Main, who died in 1873, but paved the way for Fanny to write for Dwight L. Moody and his soloist Ira D. Sankey. Thus, the stone was removed, to open a vista of opportunity to Fanny, who composed inspirational hymns used in their evangelical campaigns.

Many stories could be recounted of individuals, in differing circumstances and situations, who could give testimony to their conversion to Christ through the hymns of Fanny Crosby, which were thoroughly Bible based in their content and reached out to lost souls in their themes.

In his biography of Fanny Crosby, Woodman Bradbury states, "the theology of all these hymns is uniformly evangelical. The author believes humanity to be sinful and in need of Salvation, and she magnifies the love of God, the grace of Christ and the Power of the Holy Spirit. Fanny Crosby has tasted and seen that the Lord is good".

Francis Ridley Havergal wrote in admiration of Fanny,

> *Her heart can see, her heart can see,*
> *Well may she sing so joyfully*
> *For the King himself, in his tender grace,*
> *Has shown her the brightness of his face.*

Florence Nightingale.
(Source: public domain)

CHAPTER 8

FLORENCE NIGHTINGALE

Florence Nightingale was born to a wealthy family on 12 May 1820, and was named after the city of her birth in Italy. Florence, with her sister studied, due to their father's advanced thinking on the education of women, history, maths, Italian classical literature and philosophy. Florence was particularly academic and demonstrated an extraordinary ability for collecting and analysing data which would find its future use in later life. Florence was brought up as part of a Victorian family and thus was established in her religious beliefs and confessed in later life that she had several calls from God in which she resolved to serve God and humankind. This conviction led her to seek training for nursing, which despite quite strong reservations from the family, she pursued with vigour and determination and initially underwent a period of training at the Institute of Protestant Deaconesses in Kaiserweith, Germany.

The break from her family came in 1853 and she travelled to London to take up a post as Superintendent of the Institute for Sick Gentlemen, and was particularly successful, demonstrating her skills and knowledge in nursing care at the hospital. In October of that year Turkey declared war on Russia which gave rise to the Crimean War, and would be a turning point in the life of Florence. The London *Times* reported the dire state of wounded soldiers being treated by incompetent and ineffective medical personnel, which raised an outcry in the country.

The secretary of state for war wrote to Florence requesting her to lead a group of nurses to the Scutari, which combined with other requests were granted and Florence set out with some thirty-eight women, arriving on Scutari on November the fifth, but receiving a "not welcome" attitude from the medical personnel. Florence now faced the biggest challenge of her life, and who was going to roll away the stone?

The challenge that met Florence was not only opposition by the medical staff in the barrack hospital, but the overwhelming conditions that, described by her as the "kingdom of hell" and the lack of supplies to do the job. Florence set about overcoming these challenges with God's help, buying equipment, recruiting the wives of soldiers to deal with laundry problems, cleaning wards, and establishing basic care by properly trained nurses, also dealing with the psychological aspects that arose from conditions at the battle front.

Her patrolling of the wards at night was a feature of her dedication and devotion to the work, hence the title she became so well known for as "the Lady with the Lamp". The mortality rate was still high, and for Florence a case for concern as she battled on, despite a slow recovery from Crimean fever, which meant frequent confinement to bed with severe pain.

Florence remained at the hospitals in Scutari until their closure, before returning home to Derbyshire, to a hero's welcome, but her work in the realm of nursing was not finished.

Having developed a skill for detail recording when young, she kept meticulous records of the running of the barrack's hospitals while at Scutari, which she made available to a Royal commission leading to the establishment of the Nightingale School of Nursing at Saint Thomas's in London. The school became a model, on a worldwide basis, in public institutions for nursing education.

Florence was honoured in her lifetime by receiving the Order of Saint John and the Order of Merit, the first to receive this order. In 1910 her death occurred; at her request, a state funeral at Westminster Abbey was declined and a memorial service at Saint Paul's was performed, before being laid to rest at Saint Margaret's church, East Wellow, Hampshire. Thus ended a life of devotion to God, to her patients, to her profession and her nation.

Mary Slessor of Calabar.
(Source: public domain)

CHAPTER 9

MARY SLESSOR, CALABAR

Mary Slessor was born into a poor working-class family on 2 December 1848 in Aberdeen. The family moved to Dundee in 1859 and lived in the slums, both parents and Mary working in the mills. Her father and two brothers died leaving behind Mary, her mother and her two sisters. Her father had been a drunkard and often brought much grief to the family over many years. Her mother was a devout Presbyterian Christian, with a keen interest in missionary endeavour.

She kept track of missionary work through a magazine entitled *Missionary Record*, published by the United Presbyterian Church. By this means she encouraged young Mary to engage in activities relating to mission work. At age twenty-seven she heard of the death of David Livingstone and decided she wanted to follow in his footsteps and thus the stone was removed and opened up a vision for missionary enterprise.

Mary applied to the United Presbyterian church's Foreign Mission Board, and after a period of training, set sail on 5 August 1876 arriving at her destination in West Africa a month later. Thus, was to begin a lifetime of devoted service to her Lord and Master. After some three years of service in West Africa Mary fell ill with tropical fever and had to return to Scotland for recuperation.

Having rested and recuperated she made her return to Africa and settled in Duke Town on Mission Hill and undertook charge of the mission work alone. She lived as the natives lived, ate as the natives ate becoming as one of them, which was the secret of her influence with them.

Mary longed to go further into the interior of the inland jungle and prayed for the opportunity so to do. Mary was very concerned about the practice of abandoning twins until one day a twin was brought to her which she took in and adopted, this became the beginning of a ministry that finally resulted in the practice being abandoned entirely, thus the stone was removed and God glorified, also many lives were saved.

After a period of twelve years the Mission Board gave permission to open a mission station in the wild country of Okoyong, where the native tribes were savage and cannibals. At the village of Ekenge she opened a mission station and began transforming the lives of the natives through the Gospel. She built herself a little hut dwelling, native fashion, and thus began a ministry of changing "cannibals" unmatched by any woman missionary to the region. Mary became the greatest friend of the chief's sister "Ma Eme" who was responsible for saving Mary's life on many occasions.

Such was her influence among the natives and tribes that she settled many battles and conflicts, which arose among the hot-tempered savages, restoring calm and following her advice in settling matters.

With the board's blessing she opened a station at Ita and saw God's blessing on the work and witnessed the power of the gospel at work changing the lives of the natives as occurred at Okoyong. Mary's fame began to spread around the regions in which she laboured and opened the door to more opportunities. Officials in the country began to recognise the extent of her influence, and promoted her to positions of authority, knowing that she had the respect and esteem of the tribal heads as well as the natives of the area.

In 1912 her labours took their toll and she left the work for a period of rest in the Canary Islands before returning to her beloved country of adoption. She received many honours, one from the King of England, and continued her work until August of 1914 when World War One broke out. During that period, she contracted a fever, which gradually worsened until, watched over by Janice, one of the twins she had rescued, on 15 January she went to her Eternal Home having previously prayed, in the native Efik tongue. "O God release me".

Amy Carmichael of Donhavur.
(Source: public domain)

CHAPTER 10

AMY CARMICHAEL, INDIA

Amy was the eldest of seven siblings, being born in the village of Millisle, County Down on 16 December 1867. She attended Harrogate Ladies College in her youth and became a Christian at the age of fifteen. Her family moved to Belfast a year later and founded the Welcome Evangelical Church. Amy started a Sunday morning class for the mill girls, known as "shawlies", in the church hall in Rosemary Street Presbyterian Church (Wikipedia.org/wiki/Amy Carmichael).

Having received a call to work among the mill girls of Manchester, she then moved on to missionary work. Her vision for this work was hindered by her suffering from neuralgia, which often put her in bed for many weeks. Her initial intention was to work through the auspices of the China Inland Mission, but that was altered due to health problems, which rendered her unfit for the work. Thus, the stone seemed to be a barrier too difficult to remove. Undeterred she later joined the Church Missionary Society.

The way opened up for her to travel to Japan, but after a short period had to return home through ill health. Still pursuing her vision and calling she travelled to Ceylon (Sri Lanka), then on to Bangalore, India, where she finally found her life-long vocation. The stone had finally been removed to open up a life-long ministry to the people of India.

The story of the ministry in Dohnavur is one of amazing perseverance and compassion, in which under severe threats, even of her life, she rescued and cared for the temple children from sexual exploitation. Some one thousand or more children were rescued from what was for them, a bleak and degrading future. For the fifty or more years Amy spent in India she took in hundreds of unwanted children and became known as "Amma", or Mother, to them. An encounter with such a temple girl, called Preena, began a ministry which was to continue for the rest of her time in India.

The challenge was immense, since it was acceptable practice, in the Buddhist religion for such to take place. Amy faced great opposition but her tireless labours eventually reaped reward and led to the law in India being changed. Thus, the stone had been rolled away and a new era had opened up for the removal of child abuse.

In later life Amy had an accident which proved devastating in respect of the ministry she had developed and she spent the last twenty years of her life in bed as an invalid. Yet another stone had to be rolled away. Her incapacity led her to spending time to write many books of her experiences in India, her proving God's goodness, her increasing intimate relationship with God and her continuing ministry, despite the changed circumstances.

Amy had worked for over fifty years in India, without returning to the UK, in a remarkable life of service to her Lord and Saviour. On 18 January 1951 she passed into the presence of her Lord at the age of 83 years. A bird bath marks the commemoration of Amy and her work under a tree in Dohnavur and in Welcome, a centre named the Amy Carmichael Centre serves to remind succeeding generations of her desire to care for people, especially the poor and ill used in society.

Corrie Ten Boom, Holocaust survivor.
(Source: public domain)

CHAPTER 11

CORRIE TEN BOOM, HOLOCAUST SURVIVOR

Corrie Ten Boom was born into a family of working-class jewellers and watchmakers in the Netherlands, who lived in Amsterdam, and traded in jewellery and watches, her father being a craftsman in watchmaking. Corrie herself became a watchmaker and was the first woman to be licensed in the trade in the Netherlands. The family were Calvinist Christians and worshipped in the Dutch Reformed Church.

The Germans invaded the Netherlands in 1940 and among the restrictions imposed was that of the banning of youth clubs. One day in May 1942 a woman arrived at the doorstep, with a suitcase in hand, said she was a Jew, that her husband had been arrested, her son had gone into hiding and she was seeking refuge. Having previously helped neighbouring Jews, Casper, Corrie's father readily agreed to help as he considered the Jews to be "God's chosen People". Thus began a ministry to the Jews, that would prove both dangerous and costly to the family of the Ten Boom's.

They had specially made, a room to house such refugees, in secret, which became known as "the hiding place". Corrie and her sister Betsie opened the home to both Jewish and Gentile refugees, and this became a safe refuge to such, who were in danger of their lives because of German repression.

Guarding their secret activity became more and more difficult as time went on and, on 18 February 1944, a Dutch informant told the Nazis about the activity and they acted immediately, arresting the whole Ten Boom family. They were initially imprisoned, Corrie being put in solitary confinement and eventually both Corrie and Betsie were sent to a political concentration camp and finally to Ravensbrück, a women's labour camp.

Betsie died at the camp; fifteen days later Corrie was released, albeit due to a clerical error, but had been part of a group destined for the gas chambers. Corrie returned home and continued her work of hiding the mortally disabled who were in fear of execution from the German hierarchy. The stone had been rolled away in that she was free from the restrictions and deprivations of the labour camp, but there were still challenges to be faced as the occupation continued.

After the war Corrie returned to the Netherlands and set up a rehabilitation centre to house concentration camp survivors, also housing jobless Dutch collaborators in need of care. The amazing display of love and forgiveness could not go unnoticed, both on the local front and on a wider scope. On one occasion during her worldwide travels, making known her experiences, she encountered two German prison guards who had been employed at Ravensbrück.

Confronted by these two former prison camp guards, who had been particularly cruel in their dealings, especially to Betsie, she shook hands with them and frankly forgave them both, in the true Spirit of Christ.

In later life Corrie was given many honours for her life's work, from the Queen of the Netherlands, from Israel, and from the United States of America, by whom she was given an honorary doctorate. Corrie Ten Boom reached millions of people throughout the world with the message of the Gospel. Finally, her health failed and she settled in California where she died on her 91st birthday, on 15, April 1983 being buried in California. Her home in the Netherlands became a museum of remembrance, but her heavenly home is now her happy experience. So many stones of challenge were found in her pathway of life, but God in his goodness rolled each away to enable his faithful servant to glorify His Name.

Gladys Aylward, of China.
(Source: public domain)

CHAPTER 12

GLADYS AYLWARD, CHINA INLAND MISSION

Gladys Aylward came from a working-class family in North London, one of three siblings. She was born in 1902 on 24 February, and found employment as a domestic worker, entering into such work in her early teens. Her education was basic, attending Silver Street School in Edmonton, London. Upon being accepted by the China Inland Mission for training, she began studying Chinese but made little progress and was not offered further training. Thus, the first challenge was to end in disappointment for the eager missionary, and the stone remained in place until she heard of a 73-year-old missionary who was looking for a younger woman to carry on her work.

Gladys made contact with Mrs Lawson and received acceptance, provided she could get to China by her own means. The possibility of the stone being removed was now very much a reality, and she used her life savings to travel to China by the Trans-Siberian Railway. The journey was fraught with danger, and the war between China and the Soviet Union made it even more dangerous and meant that Gladys had to go via Japan to Tientsin and from there to Yangcheng, an overnight stop for mule caravans.

The two women set up an inn and supplied food and shelter for the caravaners taking opportunity to make known the gospel to the caravan travellers. The inn became known as the Inn of Eighth Happiness, dedicated to the eight virtues – love, virtue, gentleness, tolerance, loyalty, truth, beauty and devotion. Sadly, Mrs Lawson died and before departing requested that Gladys continue with the work.

In the course of time Gladys was appointed as an assistant to the government as a Foot Inspector, touring the country and enforcing the law against the practice of binding the feet of young children, and though she met considerable opposition, was very successful and earned citizenship of the Republic of China. Gladys returned to the UK in 1949 and, after the death of her mother, planned to return to China, but the Communist government refused her entry, upon which she went to Hong Kong and then to Taiwan.

Gladys is most remembered for saving some one hundred orphans from the Japanese during the invasion in 1938. The Japanese army occupied Yangcheng and the people were told, by the Mandarin, to retreat into the mountains. On receiving the communication from General Ley to retreat, she decided not to do so, but finally determined to flee the government orphanage at Sian, taking her children with her.

After some twelve days of hazardous journey, they arrived at the Yellow River with no means of crossing, a stone which appeared to be irremovable. Having listened to the simple faith of the children, who had said, "God can do anything" they knelt and prayed and sang. A Chinese officer heard their singing, and on enquiry, heard their story, provided a boat, and the whole company arrived at their destination safely.

The trek had proved severely demanding for Gladys, and in her exhaustion, suffering from typhoid fever, she collapsed and descended into delirium for several days. After recovering and with improved health she started a church in Sian, and set up a leper settlement in Szechuan, but the toilsome labours over the years had left her health permanently impaired, requiring a return to England for surgery and recovery. She returned to the Orient in 1955 and despite difficulties encountered she eventually settled in Taiwan where she opened an orphanage on Formosa. On 3 January 1970 she passed into the presence of her Lord and Saviour whom she served so well.

Elizabeth Elliot, missionary to the Aucas.
(Source: image used by kind permission of The Elisabeth Elliott Foundation – for further information on the life and legacy of Elisabeth Elliot visit elisabethelliot.org)

CHAPTER 13

ELISABETH ELLIOT, MISSIONARY TO THE QUECHUA

Elisabeth Elliot was born into a Christian family, being one of six children, and grew up with the Bible taking top priority within the family unit, Elisabeth trusted the Saviour at five years of age, but it was in later life that she became conscious of the need to live a life committed to the service of Christ.

At Wheaton College, Illinois she met Jim Elliot, and shared an interest in missionary work. Before they married in 1953, they both visited and worked among the Quechua Indians. In 1955 Elisabeth gave birth to a daughter, whom they named Valerie, having married in Quito in Ecuador. Both she and Jim were very aware of the risks they were taking in trying to reach the Aucas, as they had been told of the savagery of the Aucas and how fierce they were, having discussed together the possibility that the mission to reach them might end in death.

Jim, with four other Christian missionaries, were speared to death in the jungles of Ecuador by the Huaorani Indians, of whom Elizabeth had been warned. After his death Elisabeth, together with Rachel Saint, the sister of one of the other missionaries killed, decided to continue the work among the Quechua in the location near to the Auca territory.

The challenge now facing them was who was going to roll away the stone and enable contact to be made. It has often been said that man's extremity is God's opportunity, and so many, many times this has been the experience of God's servants, in difficult and challenging circumstances. At the time of Jim's death, the only link with the Aucas was a young woman named Dayuma, who had fled the tribe, to live with missionaries and had become a Christian. It was initially from her that Elisabeth and Rachel learned the culture and language of the Aucas.

In the autumn of 1959 the breakthrough came, when two Auca women left the tribe and arrived at a neighbouring settlement. These three women, Dayuma, Mintaka and Minkumo, decided to return to the tribe, and after three weeks returned to the mission compound bringing seven other Aucas with them along with an invitation to visit the tribe. Elisabeth felt that this was of the Lord, and despite the risks involved, and warnings from fellow Christians, she journeyed, taking Valerie and Rachel with her, trekking through jungle trails, as well as travelling by canoe. They arrived at a clearing in the jungle to meet a welcoming party, a friendly reception and a good relationship.

She returned, with Valerie and Rachel, and worked among the Aucas until 1963 when she returned to the USA.

The western media entered the fray, criticising the missionaries, but Elisabeth stood firm, declaring that such people are "lost without Christ". Ironically it was exposure to Western civilisation that proved detrimental to the Huaorani people, rather than the Gospel.

On her return to the USA Elisabeth engaged herself in ministry, speaking to a wide audience on mission and missionary activity, also writing a number of books about her experiences as a missionary and that of her husband Jim. The work among the Huaorani continues with believers being established and a church formed; Elisabeth married a second time and then a third time, losing her second husband in 1973. Her daughter Valerie became a pastor 's wife in 1976 raising eight children.

The testimony to this woman's faith can be summed up in the words, "we have proved beyond doubt that God means what he says – 'his grace is sufficient – nothing can separate us from the love of Christ'".

Joni Eareckson, paraplegic.
*(Image used with permission from Joni & Friends,
International Disability Center, Agoura Hills, CA)*

CHAPTER 14

JONI EARECKSON, PARAPLEGIC

Joni was born in 1949, in Baltimore, Maryland, to John and Lindy Eareckson, the youngest of four daughters, and named Joni, so her name would be pronounced 'Johnny' as it was for her father. As a youngster she was very active and athletic and at eighteen years of age had an accident whilst swimming in Chesapeake Bay, diving into shallow water, fracturing the fourth and fifth clavicle levels, and ending up as a quadriplegic (tetraplegic) being paralysed from the shoulders down.

The rehabilitation period generated a time of anger, followed by depression, suicidal thoughts and religious doubts. It seemed that the "stone" which had entered her life could never be rolled away. In the process of time Joni began to seek answers to the purpose of the accident and the subsequent paralysis, and searched the Bible for some hidden reason, but met with little light as to why and what should be her lot in life. Then God answered her prayer in an unexpected way when a young teenager, called Stephen, entered her life, and she confessed to him, "I just don't get it". For a young man Steve had a wise head and did not pretend to give an answer as to why, or for what purpose, but simply pointed her to the Lord Jesus Christ, and took her to the cross asking, "Whose will do you think the cross was?" When he stated that the active participants were doing what they did to Christ, driven by Satan, they did what God's power and will had decided should happen, the cross was "no mistake", the light began to dawn on her soul.

The battle was just beginning, the fight against the physical and that of the spiritual. The daily routine of being lifted out of the wheelchair, being put to lay down, the never-ending routines for a paraplegic, the constant depending on others, "I so often had my fill of it and mumbled to myself, 'I want to quit'. I was slowly learning that self-pity was a deadly trap". Here was another stone to be rolled away, and it was the power of the resurrection that proved decisive.

In 1979 Joni founded the Joni and Friends movement to accelerate Christian ministry in the disability community worldwide. The organisation grew rapidly and in 2006 Joni and Friends were able to establish the Friends International Disability Centre, which has four flagship programmes. Joni's work as a disability advocate has led to Presidential appointments in a number of areas and on advisory committees, furthering the work in relation to disability provision. In 1982 Joni married Ken Tada and enjoyed thirty years of marriage facing many trials and challenges, overcoming them in the strength of Christ.

Joni and Ken undertook a busy and demanding schedule on a daily basis together. Sadly, a separation took place in later years ending in divorce. Joni was to be diagnosed with breast cancer, from which she claimed to be healed only for a second diagnosis to confirm its return.

Joni came to terms with the divorce from her husband and the diagnosis of cancer and continues to pursue her activities with various organisations giving herself to the Lord and depending on His goodness and grace to sustain her.

Jackie Pullinger, missionary in Hong Kong.
(Source: public domain)

CHAPTER 15

JACKIE PULLINGER,
HONG KONG

Jackie was born in 1944, in London, and from an early age wanted to be a missionary. At that early age she had little knowledge of what being a missionary involved she was just five years of age when she heard a missionary speak at her Sunday School.

In her late teens she enrolled at the Royal College of Music, specialising in the Oboe instrument and after graduating from the RCM her overriding desire was to become a missionary. There followed the usual route of applying to missionary organisations, only to find refusal at every stage. Here was a stone she herself could not roll away, and had to face the challenge, "Who would roll away the stone"?

Jackie went and sought the advice of a local minister named Richard Thompson, and was told by him, "buy a ticket for a boat, and leave the boat at a stop where, as a result of prayer, the Spirit of God would direct her steps to the place of God's calling". This Jackie did and ended up in Hong Kong, finding a job in the city of Kowloon (the Walled City) which housed one of the world's largest opium producing centres, run by Triad gangs. Jackie made contact with gang members and leaders, and thus began a ministry to the drug addicts and opium making youths of the area.

After a period of time working in indescribable conditions, with many hazards besetting her ministry, she managed to establish a youth centre to help drug addicts and street sleepers inside the walled city. The stone had been removed and a world of opportunity opened.

Jackie started a youth club, and among those that attended were members of the Triad, rough individuals used to violence, even murder. At first, they were sceptical of this British woman who had come into their midst. With patience and perseverance Jackie continued in her ministry when many missionaries found the challenge too great and left after a few weeks or months. The gang members expected the same of Jackie, but it did not happen, in fact the very reverse was the case and she actually lived among them.

Slowly, but surely, she began to see God working in the lives of these young men, and one by one the gang members began to respond to her message and became Christians. Their future witness to friends and family also brought change into the lives of many, though some did not respond. Some experienced difficult times of withdrawal symptoms, whilst others suffered none. The impact of Jackie's ministry had an amazing effect, even on some of the dangerous gang leaders.

When the threat of revenge emerged, in regard to those boys who had left the gangs and were threatened with death, God intervened and the gang bosses promised not to bother the boys. Strange though it was, the drug bosses preferred their men and boys to be free from drugs, as in that state they could trust them more than those on drugs. The drug bosses renounced the claim on those boys who had become Christians.

In the years that followed Jackie opened several more homes, the work expanded and with the help of several American missionaries she was able to set up St Stephens Society which is still operating today.

The walled city was eventually pulled down in the 1990's but Jackie continued her work helping hundreds to a new life, free from drugs and serving Christ. Jackie continues to give her life to those in desperate situations, poor and destitute, often forgotten, but not by God, who through his servant, and preaching of the Gospel has rolled away the stone to yield an abundance of fruit for the kingdom.

Abraham and Isaac.
(Source: public domain)

CHAPTER 16

ABRAHAM, FATHER OF
THE FAITH

The New Testament states that, in the words of Stephen, the first Christian martyr, "the God of Glory appeared to our father Abraham" (Acts 7:25). This encounter was to set Abraham on a journey, where he would leave his country and kindred and head for a land which God promised he would show him.

Thus began a trek that Abraham would, in obedience to God, undertake in faith, for the testimony of scripture tells us, "he went out not knowing where he was going" (Hebrews 11:8). The first stone had been removed when he left his country and kindred. There were to be many stones that would have to be removed before he would finally reach the land which was contained in the promise.

Abraham was to break ties with, not only his nation, but from his kindred, thus we see that in Haran Terah died, and then the herdsmen of Lot fell out with the herdsmen of Abraham and the break with his kindred was finally arrived at; the separation was complete. It was at this time that Abraham was to receive assurance from God of the promise made, before leaving Ur of the Chaldees. When Lot separated himself from Abraham we read that "Lot journeyed East".

At that time God appeared to Abraham (named Abram up to that point) and said, "Lift up now thine eyes and look from the place you are at, Northward, Southward, and Eastward and Westward. For all the land that you see, to you will I give it and to your seed for ever". Once again God had rolled away the stone and all was to be Abraham's possession. Though this was only partially fulfilled and the day would come when Israel, as a nation, would be scattered to many parts of the earth, because of disobedience to God's commands, God will yet fulfil His promise to Abraham.

In regard to the land of promise and its possession. This, in terms of the world view, is a stone which is irremovable and seemingly, so big, as to be beyond possibility, but the promises of God are yea and amen, in Christ Jesus, and will be achieved in God's appointed time.

Thus the Father of Faith, Abraham, who believed God, will see the promise finally accomplished, that God may be vindicated, His promise validated and His people satisfied with His goodness and mercy.

Moses speaks to the people.
(Source: public domain)

CHAPTER 17

MOSES, THE CHOSEN LEADER

From the very early breathings of life, as a newborn baby, Moses was facing danger. Being in peril of his life because of the edict of Pharaoh, King of Egypt; this being centred on the midwives as they delivered the new-born, "if it be a son then you shall kill him" (Exodus 1:16).

Here was a challenge, a stone to be rolled away, which the midwives sought to overcome, Thus Pharaoh, issued another edict that all male children born should be, "cast into the river" (Exodus 1:22). The ineffectual position of the midwives rendered Moses open to the obedience of the Egyptian officials to execute the order of the king, but the amazing outcome was that Moses, having been placed in the very sphere in which he should have died, was in the place where he would enter a new life in the palace of the King. Thus, God had, for Moses and his family, rolled away the stone that seemed irremovable.

Many other challenges were to face Moses in the days that followed, even to him fleeing from Egypt, for a life in the backside of the desert, but a greater challenge was to come and a greater stone to be removed. An encounter with God, in the backside of the desert, involving a burning bush, was to change the whole course of his life.

"Come now and I will send you to Pharaoh, that you may bring MY PEOPLE OUT OF EGYPT," was the word he heard from God. Could such a thing be possible, could such a great stone be rolled away. No wonder Moses was so incredulous at such a prospect, and declared, "who am I that I should go"?

The task seemed unattainable, the audacity of such an aim was unrealistic, the power required to execute such a project was immense, how could this be achieved?

The secret is found in Exodus chapter 4 and verse 12, where God says, "I will be with you". It is instructive to consider what God says to Moses during this encounter:

verse 7 – "I have seen the affliction of my people"
verse 7 – "I know their sorrows"
verse 8 – "I am come down to deliver"
verse 9 –"I have seen the oppression"
verse 10 – "I will send you to Pharaoh"
verse 12 – "I will be with you"

The words recorded in Mark's gospel in regard to the stone are certainly applicable here, "for it was very great". Only our OMNIPOTENT God could remove that stone. We know the story well, God sent the plagues, God divided the Red Sea, God judged Pharaoh and his hosts, and God brought them to the edge of the promised land.

Moses was the vehicle through whom God worked. It is recorded in the book of Hebrews chapter 5 verse 2, "as Moses was faithful in all his house", a statement repeated in verse five, "as Moses was faithful in all his house as a servant". TWO, as used in Scripture, is the number of TESTIMONY, and God gives testimony to the faithfulness of Moses – His servant (see also Numbers 12:7).

Joshua encourages the people.
(Source: public domain)

CHAPTER 18

JOSHUA, THE SUCCESSOR

The commission given to Joshua was one of the great challenges of the Old Testament records. It was, we might conjecture, among the children of Israel, assumed that Moses would be the man to take them into the land of promise to possess it. NOT SO!!! For God says, "My thoughts are not your thoughts, neither are your ways MY ways" (Isaiah 55:8). God says to Joshua:

1) "Go over this Jordan, you and all the people" (Joshua 1:2).
2) "There shall not, any man, be able to stand before you" (Joshua 1:5).
3) "For unto this people you shall divide the land which I swear unto their fathers to give them." (Joshua 1:6).

All was put into the hand of Joshua – (F.B. Meyer pp14 CLC, 1977) What a challenge faced Joshua, a whole land to be conquered and divided among his people as God directed. The first challenge to be met was that of Jericho, but before the siege of Jericho, Joshua was to have an encounter with the captain of the Lord's host and heard the very words that were spoken to Moses, "Loose your shoe from off your feet, for the place on which you stand is holy". (Joshua 5:15).

What a confirmation to the servant of God, who had faithfully served Moses through the wilderness. Any doubt as to the removal of this great stone, was now removed and Joshua moved on to lay hold on the promise of God, "see I have given into your hand Jericho" (Joshua 6:2).

The story of the fall of Jericho is well-known, but the epitaph not so; the curse of Jericho, being stated by Joshua and the fame of Joshua noised throughout the country.

Much was still to be accomplished as battles faced Joshua and the people of Israel, but the presence and power of God was at the core of the successful campaign undertaken. The fall of Jericho was evidence of the presence and power of God in a remarkable way, as confirmation to Joshua of the promise given at the outset of the commission (Joshua 1:5). In that promise the "I will" of God gave supreme confidence to Joshua. "I will be with you", "I will not forsake you", and the duration of the promise was for, "all the days of your life".

The epitaph given to Joshua, by God himself, is indicative of the influence exerted by Joshua on family, and fellow travellers in the journey to possess the land, "and Israel served the Lord all the days of Joshua, and all the days of the elders that outlived Joshua and which had known all the WORKS OF THE LORD" (Joshua 24:31).

David plays the harp.
(Source: public domain)

CHAPTER 19

KING DAVID,
THE SHEPHERD BOY

Humble beginnings need not be a barrier to achievements or success, particularly if the life is given over to the service of God. Such was the case with David the shepherd boy who became King of Israel.

What initially proved to be a "stone" to be removed, was indeed a stone removed by God for this young, inexperienced but faithful shepherd boy whose trust in God was uncompromising and absolute.

Marked out by God as special, this being confirmed by his anointing by Samuel, the prophet, David had to overcome the resentment of his brothers by virtue of his position, the youngest in the family, considered of no account and only competent to look after sheep. But a day would come, in the place appointed, the valley of Elah, when all was to change and David would finally see the "stone" removed, by the power of God (1 Samuel 17:50), so David prevailed.

It is evident that God could see in David what others, particularly his brothers, could not see. (1 Samuel 16:12). The days of preparation in the wilderness caring for the sheep, would prove to be invaluable for future days as King, with greater responsibilities. The challenges that faced David in those days of kingly rule were many and varied, from within and without, from family and friends, to outright enemies seeking his destruction. Yet in all of these David never lost his trust in God, even when he failed miserably, because of self-seeking desires.

This trust in God saw many great "stones", as it were, rolled away by God's great power and amazing grace and mercy. David witnessed this and so often resorted to praise the God who had so miraculously delivered him, provided for him, and guided him in his changing journeyings.

David, when he writes in Psalm 37 is reflecting on God's goodness over the years of his life, and in verse 25 of the Psalm he says, "I have been young and now am old, yet have I not seen the righteous forsaken, nor his seed begging bread – He is ever merciful" (verse 26). As he closes the Psalm he declares "The Lord shall help them and deliver them... because THEY TRUST IN HIM" (Psalm 37:40).

Challenges overcome, barriers removed, victories gained, setbacks resolved, deliverance provided, etc., were David's constant experiences, the seemingly irremovable "stones" that barred the way by God's power were graciously rolled away to open up a new vista of opportunity for David to witness God's purposes in his life and that he might know, "the blessing of God that makes rich" (Proverbs 10:22).

William Carey, the shoemaker.
*(Source: used by kind permission of Wholesome Words –
www.wholesomewords.org)*

CHAPTER 20

WILLIAM CAREY, THE SHOEMAKER

William Carey was one of five siblings born in the village of Paulerspury in Northamptonshire. He had a special gift for languages, teaching himself Latin and later, as an apprentice taught himself Greek. Whilst working for his master Clarke Nichols he met a fellow apprentice John War who was a dissenter and through his influence formed a Congregational Church, and when Nichols died, he went to work for a local shoemaker, Thomas Old. He married his sister-in-law Dorothy Plackett who was illiterate, but had seven children with William, two daughters, who died in infancy, and a son who died at the age of five. Carey always acknowledged his humble beginnings and referred to himself as "a cobbler".

Carey later allied himself to the Baptist movement and became interested in mission work, preaching ofttimes on the subject, but meeting with resistance, until he met a certain Dr John Thomas, who had been in Calcutta and had returned to England raising funds for missionary work. The upshot was that Carey would accompany him on his return to India. Thus began a ministry that was to prove far reaching in its effects. The "stone" was now rolled away.

In 1793 Carey and his party arrived in India and met with considerable hardships, one being that the East India company was opposed to mission work. On arriving, Carey and John Thomas became managers of the indigo factories to support their families. After a few years Carey's young son, Peter, died and Dorothy began to show signs of mental illness, a condition that ultimately took her life. Yet Carey persisted through these challenges.

In 1800 Carey had transferred his activities to the colony of Serampore where he remained until his death. Carey's great gift was linguistics and he laboured to translate the Bible, and various other works, into Bengali, this being a work of great importance and a precious legacy for the Indian people. In Serampore Carey, with two other helpers, founded the Serampore College and with his helpers laboured for social reform; one particular practice of widows burning themselves on their husbands' funeral pyre he fiercely criticised and opposed. The practice ended in1829 with Carey given the responsibility of translating the government edict into Bengali and it was published straightway.

In Carey's long life he enjoyed, for the most part, good health, but on three occasions despaired of life, only to recover. Reflecting on his years of labour in India he said, "When I compare things as they are now in India, with what they were when I came here, I see a great work has been accomplished, but how it is been accomplished I know not".

On June 9, 1834, he passed on to his reward, his work had ended leaving 30 missionaries, 40 native teachers, 45 stations and approximately 600 church members; he was also the initiator of the English Baptist Missionary Society, through which thousands have been brought to Christ. A faithful and devoted servant of his Lord.

Adoniram Judson

Adoniram Judson of Burma.
(Source: used by kind permission of Wholesome Words –
www.wholesomewords.org)

CHAPTER 21

ADONIRAM JUDSON, BURMA

Adoniram Judson was born on 9 August 1788 in Malden, Massachusetts. He entered college at sixteen and graduated valedictorian of his class at the age of nineteen. Whilst studying he met Jacob Eames, a sceptic, leading to Adoniram abandoning his childhood faith. An event, which occurred whilst Judson was staying at an inn, brought about a radical change in his life, his friend Eames fell violently ill and died in the night and Adoniram discovered the tragedy the next morning. The shock returned Judson to the faith of his youth and ultimately to the dedication of himself to God. The "stone" of doubt and scepticism had been rolled away by events, permitted by God in his gracious dealings.

It was in the year 1810 that Adoniram joined a group of students who were mission minded and who were involved in the establishment of America's first organised missionary society. He was appointed to the society as a missionary to the East and after marriage to Anne Heseltine he set sail aboard the big caravan for India. They arrived in Calcutta on 17 June 1812. After a short stay the missionaries were ordered out of India, by the British East India company on 13 July 1813; Judson moved to Burma, his wife having miscarried whilst on board ship.

They settled in Rangoon where Judson mastered the Burmese language and started work on the translation of the Gospels into Burmese. In 1824 he, with his wife, transferred to Ava where he was imprisoned for two years, during which time Anne visited him every day. After his release Anne passed away. In 1827 Judson moved again to Maulmain where school buildings and a church were erected. Here he married Sarah Hill Boardman and completed his translation of the Bible into Burmese. He also compiled a Burmese grammar dictionary and a Pali dictionary.

In 1845 he returned to America due to the ill health of his wife, who passed away during the voyage. Whilst in America Judson married Emily Chubbuck, who returned with him to Burma where the rest of his life was devoted to rewriting his Burmese dictionary.

Judson had TWO master passions:

1) To translate the Bible into Burmese.
2) To lead individuals to know Christ and his transforming power.

Judson's concern was to set the gospel into the language of the other tribes and nations, and he went on extended preaching trips, to villages scattered throughout the jungles, travelling by boat to reach these remote areas.

Being a missionary meant to Judson just one thing, to join with Christians in a supreme endeavour, "to seek and to save the lost". He was a tireless seeker of souls. By the mercy of God, Judson lived, not only to translate the entire Bible into Burmese, but also to see thousands pass from darkness and death to life and immortality. In the year 1850, on 12 of April Judson breathed his last and went home to glory.

Anthony Norris Groves, Father of Faith Missions.
(Source: public domain)

CHAPTER 22

A.N. GROVES, FATHER OF
FAITH MISSIONS

A.N. Groves was born in Newton Valence, Hampshire, the only son in an Anglican family of six. He trained as a dentist and opened his practice at the age of nineteen. He later enrolled in Trinity College, Dublin with a view to ordination in the Church of England, which did not materialise. He joined himself to Christians meeting in private houses, where he met J.N. Darby amongst others, one of whom was George Muller of Bristol, who had married Groves' sister Mary. He left Plymouth to set up practice in Exeter, having met and married Mary Bethia Thompson.

While in Exeter, he enrolled as an external student in Trinity College Dublin again, with a view to ordination in the Church of England, but after studying New Testament practices of the early church he withdrew from Trinity College and continued to meet with Christian believers meeting in private houses, becoming a prominent leader in the Open Plymouth Brethren.

In 1829 Groves, with his wife Mary, and his two young sons, Henry and Frank, and accompanied by several Christian friends, one of whom was John Kitto, sailed for Baghdad. The year 1831 was a year of intense misery with plague, civil war, floods and famine in which Groves suffered the loss of his wife and recently born baby daughter. It was at this point that the way opened up for unrestricted missionary work in India, and on the invitation of Colonel Arthur Cotten, Groves decided to visit India and found many open doors for the gospel. In 1834 he accompanied Alexander Duff to Scotland to nurse him back to health, and whilst in Britain he married a second time, to Harriet Baynes who accompanied him with John Kitto, Edward Cronin, John Parnell and others, with his sons from Baghdad on his return to India. He set up a missionary team in Madras and recruited a number of missionaries to pioneer new ventures in the Godavari Delta and Tamil Nadu.

A.N. Groves, though a man of meek and humble nature, was nevertheless, a giant in his devotion to Christ and the spread of the Gospel to the lost. His influence in the lives of men of stature and academic achievement, to win them to the cause of Christ is supreme among mission endeavour, it is no false claim, made by those who knew and worked with him, that he was referred to as the "Father of Faith missions". The well-known Hudson Taylor was greatly influenced by the writings and teachings of Groves as were other missionaries of great note.

In the early days in India Norris Groves was particularly blessed with the fellowship and ministry of J.C. Aroolappan, who travelled about the villages preaching the gospel and establishing little churches. Groves applied all his inherited ingenuity in seeking to improve the lot of native Christians in India. Silk farming, coffee planting and other industries were introduced with much of his own money.

Years of anxiety and privation took their toll and he was forced to return to England. He passed away in Bristol in May 1853. The *Missionary Reporter* was published in the same year, the *Missionary Echo* and ultimately the *Echoes of Service* publications giving details of missionary work in India, China,

Africa and many other countries of the world. The hero of missionary work, entailing much sacrifice and arduous labour had left a legacy of immense worth not only to fellow missionaries, but to Christians world-wide and especially lost souls of so many tribes and peoples and nations. God's servant had laid the foundations by God's enabling, for so great an outreach, fulfilling the commission, "Go ye into all the world and preach the Gospel."

Robert Moffat

Robert Moffat of Africa.
(Source: used by kind permission of Wholesome Words –
www.wholesomewords.org)

CHAPTER 23

ROBERT MOFFAT, MISSIONARY TO AFRICA

Robert Moffat came from humble beginnings, born in Ormiston, East Lothian on 21 December 1795 and brought up as a Methodist which, proved a difficulty with his employer at West Hall, High Leigh in Cheshire, where he worked as a gardener. During this time, he applied to the London Missionary Society to become an overseas missionary, and took an interim post as a farmer at a Plantation Farm in Dukinfield, where he met his future wife, Mary Smith.

In 1816 Moffat was assigned, by the London Missionary Society, to go to South Africa, to be joined by his wife three years later and, after seven years, disrupted by warfare among the Zulu tribesmen, he settled in Kuruman where he lived for some forty-nine years, building one of the foremost Protestant missionary communities in Africa.

During that time, he mastered the Tswana language and translated the gospel of Luke, and by 1856 had completed a Twsana translation of the entire Bible. He also laboured to raise the standard of living of the African peoples by introducing improved methods of agriculture and irrigation. Many difficulties were faced in this new sphere of work among the Bechuanas, one of which was that of being the sworn enemy of the witch doctors and in the event of crises, like that of a famine caused by drought, Moffat became the scapegoat of the witch doctor. On one occasion Moffat was facing a chief, who had come with his armed men to threaten the life of Moffat with spear in hand. Moffat confronted him by opening his waistcoat and challenging the chief to spear him in the heart, giving warning that, on so doing, Moffat's companions would also depart, upon which the chief replied "These men have ten lives when they are so fearless of death", and duly departed.

David Livingstone

David Livingstone, missionary and explorer.
(Source: used by kind permission of Wholesome Words –
www.wholesomewords.org)

CHAPTER 24

DAVID LIVINGSTONE, PIONEER & MISSIONARY

David Livingstone was born in Blantyre, South Lanarkshire on 19 March 1813, the second of seven children, in a tenement building for workers in the cotton industry. He had very humble beginnings, as at ten years of age he was employed as a "piecer" working twelve hours days.

He attended Blantyre village school and lived in a family with a strong commitment to study. He began saving money to enter Andersons University, Glasgow, as well as attending lectures in Greek and Theology at the University of Glasgow and gaining knowledge in Latin from a private tutor. He later became a student at Charing Cross Medical school and qualified as a Licentiate of the Faculty of Physicians and Surgeons of Glasgow, also having applied to the London Missionary Society for missionary training.

Livingstone hoped to go to China, but whilst taking studies in medicine in London, he met Robert Moffat, and was excited by Moffat's vision for Africa; he then focussed his ambitions on Southern Africa. In 1840 he set sail for South Africa, and at the end of the year arrived at Cape Town on 18 March 1841. By the summer of 1842 he had already gone farther north than any other European into the difficult Kalahari country.

On 2 January 1845 he married Mary, Robert Moffat's daughter, who accompanied him on his journeys until health and family needs dictated the sending home of her and their four children.

Livingstone continued his journeys, sighting lake Ngami and beginning the opening up of the interior to the gospel in the midst of the Makolulo peoples, whom he considered eminently open to the gospel and missionary work.

Continuing his journey to carry out further exploration of the Zambezi he reached Quelimane in Mozambique and eventually Victoria Falls. Returning to England in December 1856 a national hero. There followed a great deal of speaking engagements and also the publishing of his book *Missionary Travels and Researches in South Africa*, followed by *Dr Livingstone's Cambridge Lectures* which aroused a great deal of interest and created the Universities Mission to Central Africa.

Dr Livingstone set out from Britain on 12 March 1858 on what was to become the Zambezi Expedition, this being infinitely better organised than his previous solitary journeys. The expedition was fraught with difficulties, both on the personal front and on the navigational front, to say nothing of the death of his wife, who accompanied him, as well as the failure of his son Robert, who never reached him, but ended up in the United States and died fighting in the Civil War.

When the British government withdrew from the expedition, Livingstone, with a small untrained crew and a small vessel, undertook the hazardous journey, of some 2,500 miles. He persevered with the project over three decades and the expedition proved to be anything but a disaster, for there followed the creation of the British Central African Protectorate (which became Nyasaland and Malawi).

His third and greatest African journey, was his quest for the source of the Nile. He left for Africa in January of 1866, his aim being the extension of the gospel and the abolition of the slave trade, but a new objective was in his mind – the possibility of finding the ultimate source of the Nile.

Once again, he met challenges as his followers deserted him, but Livingstone pressed on into central Africa. Livingstone, in his determination, reached Lake Tanganyika in February 1869, and despite illness, continued his journey. Search parties were arranged to look for him because he had not been seen for several years. In October of 1871, H.M. Stanley finally encountered him in that famous meeting, with those well-known words, "Dr Livingstone, I presume". Stanley left for England in March 1878 but Livingstone continued on, obsessed with his quest.

In May 1873 his servant found him dead, kneeling by his bedside, as if in prayer. This faithful servant and Christian missionary ventured where no previous European had previously gone, but his labours in the gospel brought many into the kingdom of God. His determined spirit brought much by way of progress to African life.

J. Hudson Taylor

Hudson Taylor, China Inland Mission.
(Source: used by kind permission of Wholesome Words –
www.wholesomewords.org)

CHAPTER 25

HUDSON TAYLOR, CHINA INLAND MISSION

Hudson Taylor was born on 21 May 1832, the son of a pharmacist and a Methodist lay preacher. He professed faith in Christ in December 1849 and committed himself to going to China as a missionary. His contact with the Plymouth Brethren, through Edward Cronin, guided and influenced his future commitment to mission work.

He studied Mandarin, Greek, Hebrew and Latin, and in 1852 he began studying medicine at the Royal London Hospital in Whitechapel. During this time, he offered himself to the services of the Chinese Evangelisation Society, as their first missionary.

Taylor left England on 19 September 1853 before completing his medical studies, arriving at Shanghai on 1 March 1854, in the middle of a civil war. He made eighteen preaching tours starting in 1855, which were poorly received. He made the decision to adopt the native Chinese dress and pigtail, thus gaining a ready audience for the gospel. In 1858 Taylor married Marie Jane Dyer, a pioneer missionary in China, and together they laboured for the Lord at a hospital in Ningbo. Due to health problems Taylor had to return to England in 1860 for furlough.

Whilst in Britain Taylor travelled extensively throughout the British Isles, speaking and telling of the needs of China. In 1865 Taylor dedicated himself to the foundation of a new society for the evangelisation of China which became known as the China Inland Mission. In less than one year they had twenty-one missionaries and raised over £2,000 pounds (equivalent to around £182,000 in 2018).

In 1866, on 26 May the Taylors set out for China with their missionary team, arriving at Shanghai on 30 September 1866, after a perilous journey in which they survived two typhoons and a near shipwreck. In 1870 Hudson suffered the loss of newly born Noel and wife Maria, and with his own health deteriorating he returned to England to recuperate. In 1872 Hudson returned to China, with his new wife Jane (Jennie) Faulding but again had to return to England due to the death of his children's caretaker Emily Blatchley.

Hudson returned to China in 1876, and some eighteen missionaries followed him and it was at this time that C.T. Studd, the famous English cricketer became a missionary to China. In 1878 Jennie, Hudson's wife returned to China and began promoting female missionaries so that by 1881 there were 100 missionaries in the China Inland Mission. Many challenges had been faced, much work had been done, despite the setbacks, many stones had been rolled away, but one major challenge was yet to arrive, that of the Boxer Rebellion in 1900, in which 58 missionaries and 21 children relating to the China Inland Mission were killed.

Taylor, though deeply distressed, refused payment for the loss of property and life and was commended by the British Foreign Office. The meekness and gentleness of Taylor's actions left a huge impression on the Chinese people. Ill health, once again, took its toll on the Taylors and they journeyed to Switzerland where they remained until Jennie's death in 1904 and Hudson's in 1905. A faithful servant of the Lord had completed his course leaving an inheritance of future ministry to China for many years to come.

Richard Wurmbrand, Voice of the Martyrs.
(Source: public domain)

CHAPTER 26

RICHARD WURMBRAND, VOICE OF THE MARTYRS

Richard Wurmbrand was born in Bucharest on 14 March 1909, of Jewish descent, the youngest of four boys. His father died when Richard was just five years old. He studied Marxism in Moscow, but after a year returned clandestinely to Romania, being pursued by the secret police and was arrested and held in Doftana prison.

He married Sabina Oster on 26 October, 1936 and both were converted to Christ in 1938 due to the witness of Christian Wolfkes, a humble carpenter. Wurmbrand was ordained twice, once as an Anglican and then as a Lutheran. His ministry began to his countrymen and to the Red Army soldiers and, due to government control of churches, began an "underground church" ministry. He was arrested on 8 February 1948 while on his way to church services.

Wurmbrand spent three years in solitary confinement, in a cell twelve feet underground, with no lights or windows. He survived by recalling details of some of the 350 sermons preached by himself, some of which are detailed in his book entitled *With God in Solitary Confinement*. He was released in 1956 after eight and a half years, and warned not to preach, but he continued his work of underground church ministry.

When he went into prison a second time in 1959, his wife Sabina was given official news of his death, which she did not believe. His sentence was to last 25 years, but in 1964 Wurmbrand was the recipient of an amnesty and negotiations by various bodies with the communist authorities, which enabled his release on payment of $10,000. Though reluctant to leave his homeland, Richard was convinced by underground church leaders to leave for another country, and he, Sabina and their son Mihai left for Norway and eventually England.

Thus began a new ministry of being a voice for the persecuted Christians in the West, and the publication of his book *Tortured for Christ*. He later moved with his family to the USA continuing his ministry for persecuted Christians. The year 1990 saw the fall of Communism in Romania, and the Wurmbrands were able to return to their homeland for the first time in 25 years.

Richard was now able to preach in many churches and also on public television. In addition, a printing facility and bookstore were opened in Bucharest, city officials offered storage facilities below Ceausescu's palace, the very site where Richard had been held in solitary confinement. Truly, God had rolled away the stone. On 11 August 11 2000 Sabina left this scene and a year later Richard also went home to glory. A faithful servant and follower of Christ went to his reward.

Billy Graham, international evangelist.
(Source: public domain)

CHAPTER 27

BILLY GRAHAM, EVANGELIST

One cannot consider evangelistic outreach and missionary ministry in the twentieth century by men of faith and commitment and not mention Billy Graham.

Billy Graham was born on 7 November 1918, on a North Carolina dairy farm. His parents were devoted Christians, who knew about hard work and discipline, and saw in their days trying and challenging times.

In May of 1934, the Christian Businessmen of Charlotte, North Carolina, held a prayer meeting at the Graham farm, praying that the Lord would raise up someone to preach the gospel worldwide. In that year Billy gave his life to the Lord at a revival meeting. He was then sixteen years of age. After graduating from high school Billy enrolled in Florida Bible Institute and began to lead a prayer meeting, and to preach at a local church as an ordained minister of the Southern Baptist Convention.

One night, when walking in the woods, he sought God's direction for his life, and found the answer, sealed by prayer, to step out in faith and go beyond intellectual doubts and questions, to do God's will. In 1940 Billy enrolled in Wheaton College, Illinois and graduated in 1943, a short time later he met and married Ruth Bell whose parents were missionaries in China. He took on a pastorate of a small Baptist church in Western Springs, Illinois. In 1945 Billy was invited to become the first full-time organiser for Youth for Christ. Four years later, whilst conducting evangelistic meetings in Los Angeles, the media began covering him, and the upshot was that meetings convened, originally for a few weeks, lasted for a month with much success.

God's word has been presented in humble sincerity to millions throughout most of the countries of the world. Extensive travel exposed many of the activities of human suffering, which brought about, through the auspices of BGEA, the initiation of the World Emergency Fund. Dr Graham stated that, "God has given us new tools to do his work – radio, films, television and telephone, electronic and visual tools, each playing their part in the expansion of our ministry".

Billy Graham's integrity has encouraged millions to heed his spiritual guidance, among them Martin Luther King, Muhammed Ali, several Presidents of the United States and many others. He was described as being one of the "ten most admired men in the world" some fifty-one times by the Gallup Organisation.

In 1992 Billy Graham suffered a set-back when he was diagnosed with a disease akin to Parkinson's. In 2007 his wife Ruth passed away and in 2013 he preached his last sermon "My hope – America", and on 21 February passed into the presence of his Lord, a faithful and well used servant of Christ, leaving a noble heritage to America and all the World.

George Verwer, founder of Operation Mobilisation.
(Source: public domain)

CHAPTER 28

GEORGE VERWER,
OPERATION MOBILISATION

George Verwer was born on 3 July 1938 and as a 14-year-old went out to a meeting in which Billy Graham spoke. As a result, he was converted and became a Christian at the age of sixteen. Within a year some 200 of his classmates became Christians.

George had a growing conviction to share the Word of God on foreign soil. He started with distribution of the Gospel of John in Mexico. He studied at Moody Bible Institute, where he met his future wife Drena. After marriage they went to Spain where, in1961, the work of Operation Mobilisation (OM) was born. Today OM reaches across the world, through the ship Logos Hope and over 6,000 people working in over 80 nations.

In the early days of reaching out with gospel literature George reverted to blending products to minimise attention from the authorities, but when a team entered Russia, they met with difficulties when George discarded a misprinted tract, which was recognised by a pedestrian, who reported the incident, which resulted in interrogation and eventual deportation. George had several meetings with church leaders throughout Europe conveying the vision, desiring that they might share in the project of OM and its global outreach. The stone as it were seemed very big and seemingly immovable.

God was once again working and in control, and the vision materialised into what is now known universally as Operation Mobilisation, where the Word of God is distributed worldwide. Through the prayer of a faithful servant of God, named Dorothy Clapp, who first spoke to George concerning the gospel of Christ and placed him on her prayer list, the seed of faith blossoming into a vast and far-reaching project for God and his Kingdom.

In 2003 George handed over the leadership of OM, but did not retire from active outreach to the lost. Today, in his mid-seventies he is still evangelising in various ways, to reach out to a world that needs Jesus. Few people have done more, in the 20th century, to mobilise for the unreached and unengaged to be reached with the gospel through literature and distribution of the Word of God.

The New Testament gives witness to the fact that it pleased God, "through the foolishness of preaching" to save them that believe (1 Corinthians 1:21). God, through his faithful servant, has so done, thus so many have been brought into the Kingdom of God, by the Word of God, which abides forever, and has been the source by which men and women, boys and girls have been "born again". (1 Peter 1:23).

Morris Cerullo, international evangelist.
(Source: public domain)

CHAPTER 29

MORRIS CERULLO, EVANGELIST

Morris Cerullo was born is Passaic, New Jersey and orphaned at the age of two. He and his siblings were placed at the Daughters of Miriam Jewish orphanage in Clifton, where he lived until he was fifteen years old. At some point he found his Christian faith. Thus, the first stone was rolled away. He went on to study at Bible college in New York, and by the age of twenty-three was running his first crusade.

Much of Cerullo's work was spent building schools of ministry around the world, involving himself in humanitarian work on a global basis, building many orphanages in Mexico and providing aid in Ethiopia. In 2011 he purchased land in Mission Valley for the building of the Legacy International Centre entirely from donations made by faithful Christians and ministries overseas. Other projects followed.

During the course of his ministry Morris Cerullo faced many accusations of fraudulent dealings by those who were resentful and anti-religion, anti-God and anti-evangelical outreach, yet he was able to overcome and continue his ministry when found to be clear of any fraud or misrepresentation.

Schools of ministry were established in many countries such as Mexico, Brazil, The Philippines, Korea, Zimbabwe, South Africa, Kenya, Nigeria, Indonesia, Netherlands and many others. During crusades he would charge some students to reach out to their countrymen, with the "written and the living word of God". He was also instrumental in founding INSP (The Inspirational Network), a television media operation for Gospel outreach on a global basis.

Cerullo's visits to the UK were often surrounded by controversy, especially in regards to his healing ministry, which saw claims of unfounded healings and were open to accusations of prejudice in regard to respect for human dignity.

Despite the many and varied experiences in his ministry, at the age of 88 Morris Cerullo passed into the presence of his Lord and Saviour, having fought the good fight of faith and finished the course. Many a sceptic considered his ministry as one of questionable claims and conduct, but one thing is certain, he spread the word of God, both written and spoken, and presented Christ as the only Saviour of mankind.

Reinhard Bonke, evangelist to Africa.
(Source: public domain)

CHAPTER 30

REINHARD BONNKE, GENERAL OF THE ARMY OF GOD

Reinhard Bonnke was born on 19 April 1940 in Königsberg, Germany, the son of an army officer. He was taken by his mother and siblings to Denmark during the evacuation of East Prussia and spent some years in a displaced persons centre. He trusted the Saviour early in life and sensed a call to missionary work in Africa. He studied at the Bible college of Wales, where he came into contact with Rees Howells, who inspired him to greater dedication to the work of God. He later met George Jeffreys who encouraged him further in his ministry and exercise.

In 1967 he began his missionary work in Lesotho and subsequently extended his work across the continent. His early endeavours were challenging, with poor response from his evangelistic efforts which, as a result of a recurring dream caused him to adopt large scale evangelism. He held large scale tent meetings, at first renting a stadium in Gaborone, followed by the establishment of the mission organisation Christ for all Nations, based in Johannesburg, with headquarters in Frankfurt. In 1984 he commissioned the construction of a tent capable of seating 34,000, which was destroyed in a storm just before a major meeting. The meeting went ahead in the open air with some 100,000 attending. The stone had been rolled away and God had proved faithful, despite the setbacks.

Bonnke went on to hold meetings and have crusades in Nigeria and Kenya, becoming known as the "Billy Graham of Africa". Bonnke announced his farewell crusade in Lagos, Nigeria in November 2017, drawing an attendance of six million people. Some of his crusades created controversy among the Moslem communities who considered his preaching as containing anti-Islamic remarks and aroused anger among the Muslim youth.

For some ten years or more visa applications were denied and his return to Nigeria was prevented, but things changed when President Olusegun Obasanjo came to power and Bonnke was regularly welcomed to the country. Once again God had rolled away the stone for the furtherance of the Gospel in the country of Nigeria.

The lasting efforts of Bonnke's ministry in Africa was testified by many eminent pastors, teachers and lecturers, as well as presidents from states and provinces throughout the continent.

His forthright declarations, based on Scripture, caused some controversy and conflict, but he remained true to his convictions, learned in early life and firmly founded on the truth of the Bible. His influence can still be felt in many areas, local, rural, urban and regional throughout Africa, in towns and city streets, to embrace the Christian message.

Reinhard Bonnke was a true visionary, forward looking and thinking, a preacher of the Gospel of Christ and a searcher for lost souls for the kingdom.

CLOSING POEM

Time after time I hear people say to me,
Why don't we see miracles, like there used to be?
I still believe in miracles, God answers when we pray,
For God was God back yesterday, and God is God today.

God can do it again and again and again,
He's the same God today as He always has been,
Yesterday, now forever, he's always the same,
There's no reason to doubt God can do it again.

You ask God to meet your need, so why not trust in him,
He has done it all before, He can do it all again,
He's willing, much more willing than I can ever say,
To perform a mighty miracle right in your life today.

God can do it again and again and again,
He's the same God today as He always has been,
Yesterday, now, forever, he's always the same,
There's no reason to doubt God can do it again.

Don Moen

ACKNOWLEDGEMENTS

Chapter	Source
1 Rahab	*Companion Bible*, E.W. Bullinger, Kregel, 1990
	A New and Concise Bible Dictionary, Author unknown, G. Morrish, 1897–1900
5 Mary Magdalene	*Jesus of Nazareth*, Maurice Casey, Bloomsbury, 2010
6 Ann Judson	*The Life and Significance of Ann Hasseltine Judson (1789–1826)*, Sharon James, (https://sbts-wordpress-uploads.s3.amazonaws.com/ equip/uploads/2014/03/SBJME-1.2-James.pdf) https://en.wikipedia.org/wiki/Ann_Hasseltine_Judson
7 Fanny Crosby	https://www.wholesomewords.org/biography/bcrosby8.html https://codepen.io/chentsuhsi/full/bRwrja https://en.wikipedia.org/wiki/Fanny_Crosby
8 Florence Nightingale	https://en.wikipedia.org/wiki/Florence_Nightingale
9 Mary Slessor	https://en.wikipedia.org/wiki/Mary_Slessor https://www.wholesomewords.org/biography/biorpslessor.html

10 Amy Carmichael   https://en.wikipedia.org/wiki/
Amy_Carmichael
https://religionfacts.com/amy-carmichael
https://www.christianity.com/church/
church-history/church-history-for-kids/
amy-carmichael-helped-the-
helpless-11634859.html

11 Corrie Ten Boom   https://en.wikipedia.org/wiki/
Corrie_ten_Boom

12 Gladys Aylward   https://en.wikipedia.org/wiki/
Gladys_Aylward
https://womenofchristianity.com/
missionary-women/gladys-aylward/

13 Elisabeth Elliot   https://www.inspirationalchristians.org/
evangelists/elisabeth-elliot-biography/
Heroes of the Faith, October 2016,
New Life Publishing
www.elisabethelliott.org

14 Joni Eareckson   https://en.wikipedia.org/wiki/
Joni_Eareckson_Tada
http://www.joniearecksontadastory.com

15 Jackie Pullinger   https://en.wikipedia.org/wiki/
Jackie_Pullinger

17 Moses   *Moses, The servant of God*, F.B. Meyer,
Morgan and Scott, 1938

18 Joshua   *Joshua*, F.B. Meyer, CLC, 1977

19 David   *Golden Thread Series*, A. Jenkins,
Grosvenor House, 2020

20 William Carey

21 Adoniram Judson   www.wholesomewords.org/missiongiants
1610judson2.html
enwikipedia.org/adoniramjudson
www.wholesomewords.org/missions/b
judson21.html

22 A.N. Groves	https://www.brethrenarchive.org/people/anthony-norris-groves/ https://en.wikipedia.org/wiki/Anthony_Norris_Groves
23 Robert Moffat	www.bu.edu/missiology/missionary-biography/l-m moffat-robert https://en.m.wikipedia.org/wiki/robertmoffat https://www.brittanica.com/biography/robert moffat https://www.wholesomewords.org/missionary/bmoffat 10.html
24 David Livingstone	www.brittanica.com/biography/david livingstone https://en.wikipedia.org/wiki/davidlivingstone
25 Hudson Taylor	https://en.wikipedia.org /wiki/hudson taylor
26 Richard Wurmbrand	https://en.wikipedia.org/wiki/richardwuirmbrand https://www.torturedforchrist.com/about/whowas-richardwurmbrand https://israelmyglory.org/article/the-story-of-richardwurmbrand
27 Billy Graham	billygraham.org.uk/billygrahamstory www.biography.com/religiousfigures Billy Graham
28 George Verwer	https://wiki2.org/en/georgeverwer https://www.georgeverwer.uk/contact-and-bio https://stories.om.org/recent-stoty/r52107 https://www.thegospelcoalition.org/blogs/justin taylor/georgeverwer-conversion-60-years-ago

29 Morris Cerullo   https://www.sandiegouniontribune.com/
orbituaries/story/ 2020-07-13/
orbituarymorriscerullo-931-2020-fele
https://www.patheos.com/blogs/
freethinkers/2020/07/christianfriends-
morriscerullo is-alive-and-well

30 Reinhard Bonke   https://www.bloc.bbc.600vk/newsworld-
africa50781193
https://en.wikipedia.org/wiki/reinhardbonke
https://reinhardbonke.com
https://www.cfan.org.uk

CPSIA information can be obtained
at www.ICGtesting.com
Printed in the USA
LVHW032317260122
709354LV00008B/1008